# My Women, My Monsters

*Written and illustrated by*

# Janet Kozachek

*Finishing Line Press*
Georgetown, Kentucky

# My Women, My Monsters

Copyright © 2020 by Janet Kozachek
ISBN 978-1-64662-142-2 First Edition
All rights reserved under International and Pan-American Copyright Conventions. No part of this book may be reproduced in any manner whatsoever without written permission from the publisher, except in the case of brief quotations embodied in critical articles and reviews.

ACKNOWLEDGMENTS

An unpublished manuscript with illustrations was registered with the copyright office on February 23, 2016. Registration Number: TXU 2-004-146. Artist retains copyright to illustrations.

A selection of poems and illustrations in this text were previously included in the exhibition, *A Gaze Upon Woman: The Drawings of Janet Kozachek*, at South Carolina State University, Orangeburg, South Carolina, 2013. Curated by Ellen Zisholtz.

I would like to thank everyone who inspired, participated in, offered advice for, and appreciated this illustrated volume of poetry. Firstly, I am grateful to my husband, Nathaniel Wallace, who has been my most ardent fan and supporter. I would also like to thank my friend and fellow artist, Kristina Miller, who not only provided excellent formatting in her PDF files, but encouraged me to finish four poems and illustrations that otherwise would have been abandoned. A special thanks goes to Melody Jackson, for her vision of the African Cyclops and for her advice on oceanic iconography, and to A.J. Bodner for inspiring the idea for the work.

Publisher: Leah Maines
Editor: Christen Kincaid
Cover Art: Janet Kozachek, *Monstrous Transformations*. Oil on Panel.
Author Photo: Giordano Angeletti
Cover Design: Elizabeth Maines McCleavy

Printed in the USA on acid-free paper.
Order online: www.finishinglinepress.com
also available on amazon.com

Author inquiries and mail orders:
Finishing Line Press
P. O. Box 1626
Georgetown, Kentucky 40324
U. S. A.

# Table of Contents

Introduction

My Women, My Monsters ................................................................ 1

The Queen of Bones ........................................................................ 2

Crow .................................................................................................. 3

Mummified ....................................................................................... 5

The Duchess of Lists ....................................................................... 6

Subclinical Harpies ......................................................................... 8

The Empress of Clones ................................................................... 9

Titan ................................................................................................ 11

Lady Joy Killer ............................................................................... 12

Tomb Guardians ............................................................................ 14

The Guenell Lioness ...................................................................... 16

The Princess of Attachments ....................................................... 18

Succubus ......................................................................................... 19

Twinkle Tinsel Toes ....................................................................... 21

Mother Puffer ................................................................................. 23

Goddess of Rock and Wind ......................................................... 26

Wife of Polyphemus ...................................................................... 28

Daughter of the Fire Breathers .................................................... 29

Nana Necrosis ................................................................................ 30

My Monster, Myself ...................................................................... 31

# Introduction

This small volume of poetry began as a Facebook query. A gentleman who started a chat group to discuss men and women posed a question as to why there were little to no female monsters in American Culture. I gave him several examples of choice monsters of the feminine persuasion and then quipped that if they were not enough I would have to create more. Over time a book illustrating ignominious female beings issued from my ebony pencils. The verses to describe them followed.

In the end, I would have to say that my Facebook friend was probably correct about female monsters not being fully represented by American culture, for I found that my renderings often came from the myths, folklore, and literature of other times and other places. The White Bone Demon of China most assuredly influenced the creation of "The Queen of Bones." My several years steeped in the culture and language of China certainly made its mark not only in content but in my illustration style as well. A "chicken-legged terror," was influenced by the Russian Baba Yaga. Harpies hailed from ancient Greece, as did the Titan and Polyphemus. And then, of course, there was the Indian Kali. In retrospect, cultural influences included literature as well. I saw the sinister feminine depicted in the novels of Emile Zola, that I so ardently devoured in my youth, thread its way through my late verses.

When I first started writing *My Women My Monsters*, I gave my sister a look at the works in progress. She made an interesting comment about them. Family members can always be counted on to point to the very crux of problems—be they ethical or aesthetic. "I can't figure out," she mused as she read about giant crows, bone queens and terrifying chickens, "Whether you love them or hate them." "Both." I replied, hoping not to be asked for an explanation or justification of my response until I could figure out the answer myself.

The answer to my sister's question may be that it is fundamentally human to keep love and hate on the same page. If other cultures of times past and foreign lands recognized this more clearly than contemporary Americans, then perhaps it is apropos in our age for an American artist to illustrate the dichotomy. Might not an avenging savior to some be the destroyer of others? Suffice it is to say that the grace and protection of women as well as their enormous monstrosity co-exist in this small group of poems. I love them and I hate them.

—Janet Kozachek

Behold
the chicken-legged terrors
who peck their way through men's minds
and scratch on down to fear

No mellifluous voices when they speak
but croaks and shrieks
from gaping mouths
that fill the world with dread

No beauties in slumber
awaiting a lover's kiss
but wide-eyed Kali-driven madwomen
screaming out in battle cries

No thighs to fold in pleasure
but a chute for birthing trouble
Rapacious devourers of men's hearts
These are my women
These are my monsters

## My Women, My Monsters

Behold
the chicken legged terrors,
who peck their way through men's minds,
and scratch on down to fear.

No melodies mild when they speak,
but croaks and shrieks
from gaping mouths,
that fill the world with dread.

No beauties in slumber
awaiting a lover's kiss,
but wide-eyed Kali driven madwomen,
screaming out their battle cries.

No thighs to fold in pleasure,
but a chute for birthing trouble.
Rapacious devourers of men's hearts.
These are my women.
These are my monsters.

## Queen of Bones

In fleshless fury,
she casts her white bones
into the blackness of a night sky.
Ivory fingers pierce the darkness,
cutting through clouds with scapular precision.

Thing of curious wonder.
Thing of ethereal beauty.
She comes to slice through the
duplicities of men—
The Queen of Bones.

Xylophone mysteries
issue from her osteo- clatterings,
clinking within cool zephyrs.
No skin awaits touch.
No sinews muffle sound.

Thing of solemn splendor.
Thing of venerable awe.
A flash of illuminated truth—
The Queen of Bones.

She brushes aside her flowing cape,
revealing messages etched like scrimshaw
upon her jagged points and rounded condyles.
No rippling muscles to hide behind.
No fat to rest a lie upon.

Thing of quiet revelation.
Thing of sighing veracity.
laying bare the answers to who is who
and what is what—
The Queen of Bones.

## Crow

Crow watches you
with eyes you cannot see,
black on black against the setting sun,
waiting in quiet silhouette upon a branch.

Crow seeks you
in benevolent predation,
to feed upon your sorrows,
and swallow your regrets.

Crow finds you
alone among the living,
lost within memories of departed souls
who call and call your name.

Crow grasps you
in her claws folded
tight around your waist,
her black beak cool against your face.

Crow knows you
when you cross the bridge
into that great void
and come back home again.

**Mummified**

She sits in unaccustomed reticence
as a  faceless Buddha.
With her eyes, her nose, her mouth
wrapped over in sheets of woven bronze,
the breath of life turns inwards.

Her body, covered with  square plates of armor
sewn together with wires of steel
rests immobile.
Pink and blue copper tesserae
bejewel and protect her expansive thighs—
thighs swollen like the roots of trees
grown thick to support a trunk so tall,
so heavy  in that small patch of earth.

Metallic rectangles wrap her thin arms,
bound fast to her still torso.
Hands bundle into small triangles,
so that she cannot reach,
nor can she grasp.
Yet she speaks
through those small hands,
pointed lotus buds
on either side of an entrance and exit
that whispers what a mouth could never tell.

### The Duchess of Lists

The Duchess of Lists taunts you
with a roll call of things undone,
deeds gone unacknowledged,
malefactions unpunished,
absolutions never granted,
and obligations never met.
She makes pointed exhortations
that you finish soon and swiftly
these items on her lists.
Nagging hag, she follows you
in your race to complete
the goals she sets.
"Faster, faster," she cries,
"More and more."

The Duchess of Lists
is the sorceress of the clock's hours.
She ties strings to your ankles,
adding weights for good measure
that hold you back to slow you down
as she speeds up time.
She mocks your efforts to catch up.
Malicious, vindictive, her cackling cry
stings your ears and pricks your skin
with penetrating cruelty.
"You should do this," she scolds,
" you should do that," she warns.
before the sun sets on your given day.

Your exhausted and weary self
 crawls finally across her finish line,
her list held feebly in your hand,
her expectations scratched off
with thin unbroken pencil lines
and check marked here and there.
No congratulations come your way.
No "job well done" issues from her lips.
The Duchess of Lists, laughing with wicked glee,
holds up a paper proclamation.
Pointing to the items one by one,
she enumerates the things you really should have done.

**Subclinical Harpies**

Five oh nine!
A small explosion breaks the silence of a sleepless night.
Was it gun fire?
Or was it the crackling of paper unfolding?
A cautious crowd gathers.
"What is she writing?"
An angry onlooker queries suspiciously.
"She's writing about us!"
The woman with extra girth exclaims,
and in a roundabout way
she looks askance at her companions.
A motley crew of bad memories,
they fear the quiet that resurrects the past
and live in terror of the stillness
they find in uneventful nights.
Subclinical Harpies come alive then—
to usurp the peace of somnolence
that daybreak does not return.

**Empress of Clones**

Like a virus,
she enters the cells of others' consciousness,
creating clones of herself
from their bodies and their minds.
She subverts their tastes
their likes, their dislikes.

Hapless creatures
of her gene machine,
they believe what she believes.
They love her loves and hate her hates,
and hope for the culmination
of her desires—
which now are theirs.

She uses the very machinery of their being,
insidious, odious thing,
to manufacture mirrors of herself,
reflecting multiples of her visage.
Co-opting the essences of other selves,
she replaces them with her own.

The Empress of Clones dissolves identities,
Supplanting them with designs
stamped upon her clones—
leaving the indelible imprint of her persuasion.
Again and again and again,
with insatiable persistence
she releases them to do her bidding.
Out into the world her clones disperse,
strutting and posturing at her command,
their tongues speaking her language,
their hands upon their arms
copying  relentlessly her gestures.
They march in mindless synchrony.

In legion force her cloned ladies follow,
saying "Yes Ma'am," "No, Ma'am" and
"How very right you are Your Highness."
Laughing her laugh, sneering her sneers.
They toss their heads as she tosses hers,

agreeably sick with the contagion of her personality.

Contagion grows exponentially,
as clone upon clone upon clone
infect the willing, the culpable, and the vulnerable
with visions that insinuate their way
into their inner workings.
And the Empress of Clones smiles at her conquest of souls.

**Titan**

Her blank face shines out like the moon
illuminating the night sky.
Her hair traverses the glowing disk
like strands of black floating clouds,
or a celestial horse's tail
whipping out across the heavens.

She expands.
Easing her large foot forward,
she presses outward—
away from the confines of her horizon
and beyond the boundaries
that men of reason take comfort in.

Her arms, like chops of mutton,
stand rigid and upright—
the weight of a giant upon them.
She leans in contrapposto determination.
Titan over earth and sky.
Land to body and body to land.

### Lady Joy Killer

She is the mud print upon
the tiles on a freshly cleaned floor.
She is the splatter of ink
from a leaking pen
that smears across a crisp,
white piece of paper.
She is the spot of red sauce
on a newly purchased shirt.
She is the mold that damps off the hope

of a freshly sprouted seed
reaching towards the sun.
She is the Lady Joy Killer.

Lady Joy Killer intrudes
in tall black boots,
her uninvited shining buckles
glaring like the headlights
on a night road.
Her stiletto heels scrape the floor,
making an unwelcome squeal
that turns all heads and eyes
to look upon her as she bids them,
"Look my way and hear me speak."

She sees them through the site
in the lens of her left rifle eye,
her focus narrowed in upon:
the twenty-five percent who die young,
the twenty-five percent who cheat,
the twenty-five percent who steal,
and the twenty-five percent who lie.
In her statistical calculation
they are the totality of her world,
neatly divided into four quarters
in the cross within the circle
through which she peers.

Taking aim,
she sites them.
In a single blast,
she obliterates all who claim
that their antitheses also exist.
She decries their sanguine hopes,
smashes their rosy memories
murders all that is joy.

## Tomb Guardians

Their eyes bulge out in threatening stares,
eyebrows knitted in consternation.
Armored mono-breasted Amazons
guard the tombs of their fallen,
so that common folk
may never gaze upon the sheltered dead.
Protectors of eternal rest,
they slumber not themselves.
The Guardians create a disturbance,
lest their sacred departed ones be disturbed,
where they lay against their jewels
and magic objects
imbued with the power to carry
them far, away, and away—
to resplendent valleys for wandering spirits.

Guardians of the tomb
wave their upraised fists wildly on winged arms.
They frighten away the ordinary
waking wounded who
would dare to trespass
onto hallowed grounds.
Their mouths agape,
they poise to hurl invectives
against thieves of votive offerings.
They frighten all
who would desecrate
still and quiet bodily remains,
or pillage the recesses
within sanctified walls
where the motionless and helpless
lay wordless yet fiercely defended.

**The Guenell Lioness**

They called her monster,
for she sported a lion's head
upon her mighty shoulders,
turned to guide her view northward,
as her torso faced the east.
Does she stride?

Or is she dancing?
With pride and determination
she glares outward and onward
over the point of a jutting elbow.

She glides on padded hips
that hide a femininity
of imagined proportions.
Like the haunches of a feline
tightened by the sight of prey,
her massive thighs
advance upon the unwary.
Is she man?
Or is she woman?
She wears a womanly bodice
of masculine proportions.

They called her animal,
for she was born of nature
but had no mother.
Nor had she feet to walk upon
but a set of disappearing paws.
Is she beast?
Or is she person?
In her feline head
her perspicacious eyes
gaze undistractedly onward.

They called her hands a fighter's,
for they were pressed together
in tight fists across a muscled chest.
Swelled out with charismatic being,
she was a warrior moving eternally
forward into battle.
Was she guided by the blare of trumpets?
Was she marching to the beat of drums?
With steadiness and self assurance
she steps ahead.
Does she spring free as giant
from the cradle of civilization?
Or is she captive, small,
and cradled in the palm of ownership?

## The Princess of Attachments

She knows no boundaries,
holding sway over all in her dominion.
She is bound to them and them to her.
The Princess of Attachments
saunters forward,
her skin glistening with adhesive slime
that sticks to all she moves upon.

A syrup issues from her breasts,
oozing with sap-like viscosity
from the swaying pendulous forms,
bloated like the udders of a cow.
She encourages the young to suckle there.
Glued fast, they never leave
and she never lets them go.

She knows to move slowly,
edging closely to her peers.
Heedless to her encroachment,
they are unprepared for the moment
that she slides against their unprotected bodies,
sealing them to her sides
so that they can never walk away.

The Princess of Attachments
generously imparts her troubles,
 conniving to unearth the woes of others.
She exchanges ties like laces intertwined.
"We are bonded now,"
She lisps in atonal breathlessness ,
as she tightens a convoluted knot
in a kerchief across mouths
that can never utter a protest.

Her tree toady fingers
caress a dewy face,
leaving round pock marks
from the moist suction of her hands.
Fingers take, bond, absorb
the other into one within her flesh.

## Succubus

She plots in secrecy,
hiding in the cool fold
on the other side of your pillow.
She creeps stealthily out at night
to find you in your sleep.

She is a tiny thing,
a succubus deftly sliding into
a nose, an ear,
or any other orifice
that serves an easy porthole.

On minuscule legs that
propel her forward,
she enters you.
Her eager stinger
fills with venom.

She nestles deep
in your interior,
sustained by the blood
and digested food
of her host.

Slowly, so as not to break your slumber,
she injects her poison.
Like a drug from a syringe
its contents are dispensed
in cruelly calculated increments.

She paralyzes dreams
with venomous haunting.
You cannot run from terror
that settles like precipitated lead
in your stiffened muscles.

You cannot cry out your fears.
Her venom makes you mute.
You cannot reach for help.
She numbs your grasping hands
and binds your fingers closed.

You awaken with her still inside.
Parasitic succubus,
she infuses your blood with
caffeinated anxieties—so that you know
the terror of possibilities.

No splendid vistas
greet you as you rise.
You know only the height
from which to fall,
crashing to an ignominious end.

Enclosures offer no safety—
only entombment.
Your very inhalations
suck the oxygen
from life-giving air.

Succubus poison
makes the heart beat faster
and the hands shake violently
at the thought of going anywhere,
doing anything, or meeting anyone.

Behind every smile
there is a possible axe murderer.
A proposal is a con artist
attempting to steal your money
and make you homeless.

Succubus drugs your blood,
excites your nerves,
and takes you to a place
where all boats sink, all planes crash
and traffic transports you to accidents.

Until one night,
as you sleep unguarded,
she leaves your body.
Passion outweighs fear
and awakens to daring dreams.

**Twinkle Tinsel Toes**

The Twinkling Tinsel Toe Fairy
arrives in a puff of glitter.
Dressed in white chemise,
bedecked with tiny silver bells,
her pink rose petal lips part seductively.
She smiles through pearly teeth
trimmed in iridescent gold.

Twinkle Tinsel Toe Fairy loves
the dreams of the impressionable.
She dances in pirouettes upon their heads
and throws starry dust into their eyes—
crooning to them that all can be had
for the simple wishing for it
and that belief in her magic makes it so.

With a touch of her wand
the semi-literate believe that
they are educated men and women
of a lettered meritocracy.
Fairy applauds their self-esteem
as they frame their imagined accomplishments
and hang them on a wall.

Twinkle Tinsel Toe Fairy
exhorts the penniless to reside in mansions
filled with the stuff of their dreams.
Imbibing in the milk and honey
of their wide-eyed desires—
they settle in to comforts
purchased by hope and air.

She tells the average
to shoot for the stars.
The world is for their taking she says,
and greatness is within their grasp.
They dance, they sing in center stage
for audiences silently watching
only each other in mirrors.

Twinkle Tinsel Toe Fairy
informs the dying that they
have decades of healthy life ahead.
She tells them to have faith in her.
Their blood will be cleansed,
their tissues purified,
and pain will never be.

Her fee is small for such largess,
She chortles in falsetto.
Gathering her followers,
she raises her sparkling wand.
She cheers their illusions,
applauds their delusions, then waves a hand...
and "poof" they all are gone.

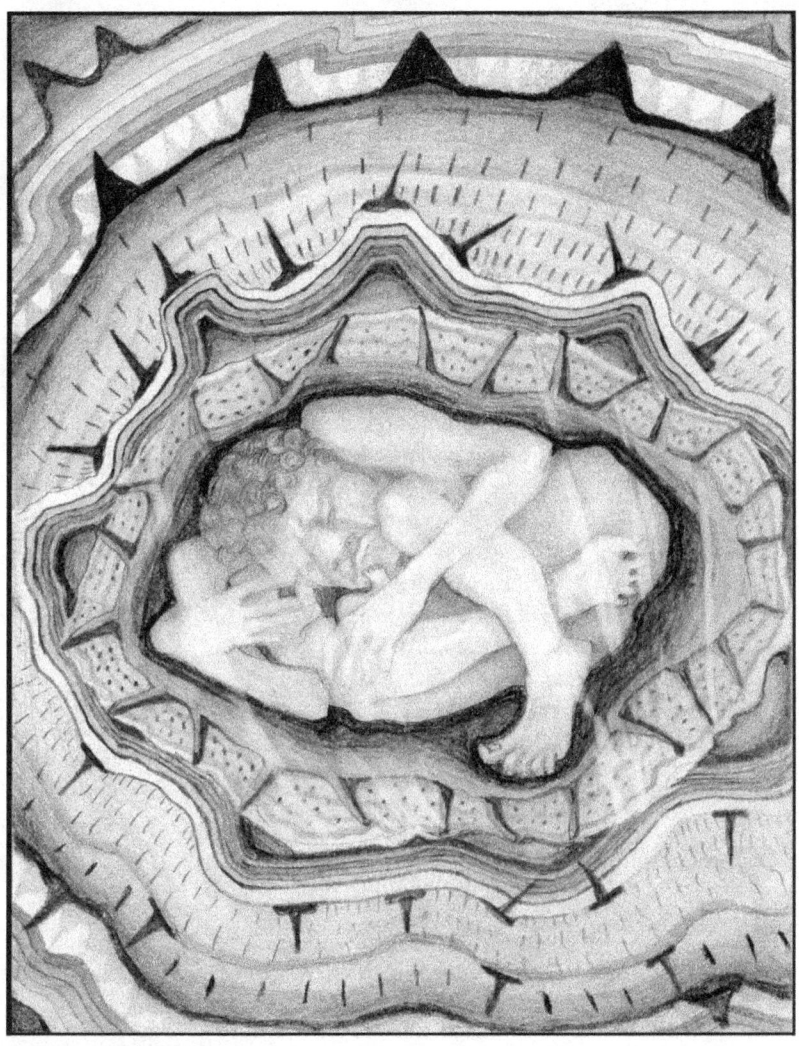

**Mother Puffer**

With every wrong perceived she expands,
filling her interior with the air of past and present sins,
meticulously counting them as they enter...
the one time you did that
the other time you said this
the last time I saw you didn't do that
the next time you should have done this.
Mother Puffer grows larger and larger
in a balloon of discontents distending
beneath her thinning skin.

She is silent but knows
it is a myth that quiet things are happy,
a lie that silence is peaceful,
and a mistake to think that a still cat is not waiting
to pounce upon its prey.

Mother Puffer enlarges,
translucent and shining like a pregnant belly.
You who have wronged me will suffer soon.
She ruminates upon the little hurts
she guides into her interior.
Like tacks and pins
that poke her skin and stick her tongue,
they inflame her more and more.

Mother Puffer swells,
like a ball of spores waiting to disperse.
She reaches the limit
she can contain within her straining walls.
Something, anything,
brushes against the coiled madness.
It splits without warning,
with the barest slightest touch,
against every living being in her midst.

Mother Puffer explodes.
The hurt held in
becomes the pain expelled,
in projectiles of razors, tacks and nails.
Like Pandora's box of wicked plagues,
they curse the world,
and all the living contained therein.
They care not who they wound
with their cuts, their scrapes
and their searing punctures,
hurling ever outward.

**Rock, Wind**

Woman of earth,
seated as a rock
spun a cyclone in her arms,
whipping air into a windy spiral
of a tornado that never quite touched down.

A histrionic whirling of her upper limbs
stirred the currents of the atmosphere
and beat a pathway across the heavens.
A passage coursed intently downward,
ending abruptly on stationary ground.

Woman of the air,
descended from the sky,
resting as a lichen covered boulder.
A cold stone against the blue horizon,
she is unmoving yet growing in strength,
static against the swirling of her dervish torso.

Rocks strewn like Jurassic eggs
punctuated the land upon which she sat.
She folded her feet beneath her hips of stone,
carved from gusts of unending wind
and shaped by the ceaseless flow of waters.

### Wife of Polyphemus

Oh! The dreaded locks
 coil over her face of bronze
and wrap around her monolithic eye—
that one staring, penetrating eye.

She is the wife of Polyphemus,
the one-eyed beastly one.
She shares his every point of view :
that one point of view,
that only idea,
the  single solution to every problem
and solitary answer to every question.

She fiercely protects his tunnel vision,
a telescope through which the world is known.
She stares out frozen,
petrifying  the perspective of the other.

Wife of Polyphemus.
She rolls that one round eye
in a slow spin clockwise to mortify,
then counterclockwise to horrify.
No pleading supplications for her.
No bargaining or cajoling
will ever change her mind, her eye.

**Daughter of the Fire Breathers**

Seated on an ancient throne,
she nourishes the embers
smoldering in her belly.
After steady inhalations
from the bellows in her breast...
Haaaaaaaaa...
she exhales a force that kindles
Fire!

Fire breather.
Her father was one.
Her mother was one, too.
A genetic gift or hereditary curse—
 she does not know.
She exhales a glowing torch
as an emblazoned answer
to questions deemed impertinent.

A flaming parrot as her familiar
perches high above her head,
cloaked in feathers carved like Scythian gold.
Holding a soot black tea pot in her ebony hand,
She cooks its contents with a breath of blaze...
Haaaaaaaaaaa...
smoking out the unprotected.

Daughter of the fire breathers–
Her charcoal face, her blackened limbs
store the energy of the ignited past
and the flames of yet-to-come.
With sparks of vengeance in her eyes...
Haaaaaaaaa...
she scorches earth, burning the unbeloved.

**Nana Necrosis**

She tucks her arms beneath her belly,
 shielding herself against the adulterants
of the outside world.
Nana Necrosis creates an anaerobic hollow,
a protected pocket of sealed off air.
What once burned now smokes,
sending black ribbons in to the sky.
Offerings of sooty bits and pieces
rise in their upward journey.

Hands that once gave life
have life pulled from them—
extracting in their turn
the will in the world.
Nana Necrosis sucks oxygen
away in a chemical sleight of hand.
"It will never work,"
and "It can't be done,"
are her daily mantras.

Explanations are not proffered.
nor can they be ascertained.
Nana Necrosis keeps her mouth obscured
and her eyes closed.
She is still and inscrutable
 behind her biomorphic massiveness.
The mysteries of her inner workings
remain shrouded.
Transformed, degraded, or merely decomposed?

**My Monster, Myself**

They poke at me.
With fingernails sharpened like little blades,
they prod me to jump
forward in my seat from the sting.
Not a big thing—
just a small shock to keep me restless on a quiet night,
with a body that wants to sleep but legs that need to walk.

Monstrous things.
Greedy hands grasp
with a strangulating hold that terrifies.
Accusing, pointing fingers,
digging digits  unearth all
that desires to silence memory.
I point back at them but they persist.

The vindictive phalange of overly sagacious females
eject a force that flows in my direction, crying out,
"You, you, you!
"You wicked thing!
Narcissus was no match for your self-indulgent gaze."

I grab for them.
They hold me back.
I press them down with a cupped hand,
and pummel them back into the earth with my fists.
They claw their way back to the surface,  nevertheless.
plucking words off the tip of my overturned tongue,
and pinching off small bits of unconscious reveries
between their thumbs and forefingers.

I look for a switch to pull to make them disappear.
I feel for a button to press to eject them from my presence.
They clap their hands together and snap their fingers
to make their presence known to me, snarling,
"It is not us, but you, you you,

You monstrous little thing!"
Their hands hold mirrors to my face and bid me look,
to study carefully my twists and turns, my almond eyed gaze.
I look at all that emanates from this backwards beast of a woman.
I see what they point to, I hear what they tell me.
I see my monster, I know myself.

**J**anet Kozachek has led an eclectic career as a writer and visual artist, pursuing education and work in Europe and China in addition to the U.S. Following undergraduate studies in natural sciences and visual art at Douglass College in New Jersey, she was the first American to matriculate at the Beijing Central Art Academy (CAFA), where she studied painting, poetry, and calligraphy. At CAFA, she found that poetry was an integral part of painting, enhancing both meaning and joy. These Asian art forms have had a lasting impact on her work.

After China, Ms. Kozachek taught in the Netherlands for the University of Maryland, overseas division. During this interval, Ms. Kozachek worked on translating poetry and researching ancient Chinese scripts while also studying ceramic art in Maastricht. She traveled across Europe, visiting historic towns, archeological sites, and museums.

After returning to the United States she entered the M.F.A. program in painting at the Parsons School of Design. During graduate studies at Parsons, Janet Kozachek studied painting and drawing with Larry Rivers, Paul Resika, Leland Bell, and John Heliker, as well as poetry with J. D. McClatchy. It was this brush with McClatchy, Yale Review editor and author of *Painters and Poets*, that first inculcated the idea for Kozachek that painting and poetry could emanate from the same creative sources in both western and eastern understanding.

In South Carolina, Janet Kozachek embarked on a peripatetic career as an occasional adjunct professor and as an artist-in-residence teaching Chinese art and Mosaics. Inspired by her study of mosaic art in Ravenna and other sites in Italy, Janet Kozachek was a co-founder and the first president of the Society of American Mosaic Artists. She wrote for and assisted with editing the society's quarterly publication, *Groutline*, and co-authored the catalogue for the first national exhibition of mosaics in the United States. She also wrote for *Evening Reader* Magazine, publishing essays on art and social issues. Her series of one hundred and thirteen small, square figurative paintings became the basis for *Moments in Light and Shadow* (currently in manuscript). Selected poems from *Moments in Light and Shadow* have been published in *Undefined* and *Ekphrasis*.

Ms. Kozachek has previously published *The Book of Marvelous Cats*, a collection of poems and illustrations with feline content. The present work, *My Women, My Monsters*, was written and illustrated for the most part during her convalescence from a protracted illness, when she found that working on small, detailed drawings provided distraction from pain and disability.

www.ingramcontent.com/pod-product-compliance
Lightning Source LLC
LaVergne TN
LVHW041602070426
835507LV00011B/1263